How to Ask a Girl Out

By
Kimberly Peters

For 26Ways.com

All Rights Reserved – 2015 –
26Ways.com

Disclaimer

This book is design to be used as an information resource only. It is not designed to be used as a definitive process for asking any specific individual for a date. Every person is different and every situation is different as well. The reader of this book assumes total responsibility for the use or application of any or all parts of this book. The writers, publishers and distributors of this book assume no responsibility for any or all of the content contained within.

Contents

Introduction	4
Who & Why?	6
Do not Be Afraid or Intimidated	8
Gauging Interest	11
Doing a "Self Audit"	16
Adopt a Positive Body Language	20
Always be Respectful and Courteous	24
Discovering Common Ground	26
Breaking the Ice	30
Interact with Her	33
Help Her Out	36
Smile When You See Her	38
Look Your Best	40
When You Can Date Without Asking Her!	43
Ask Her in Private	46
Create a Low Risk First Date	49
Keep it Light, Fun and Pressure Free	53
Make the Date Mostly About Her	56
Be Honest!	59

Who Pays?	61
After Date Follow-Up	64
Why Rejection is No Big Deal	67
Dating Tips, Hints & Suggestions	70

Introduction

There are few things in this world more nerve racking for guys than having to ask a girl out on a date. All kind of questions and fears run through our minds and some of us become so afraid and paralyzed by that fear that we wind up not doing a damned thing. So we either hang out with friends, or even worse, eat alone and go to the movies alone.

The great thing is that you do not have to be afraid and you can be successful in getting women to go out with you. It's not hard and we don't want you to do anything other than be yourself! We don't want you to pretend to be someone you are not. If you want to meet the right girl and create a long term relationship, then honesty is always the best policy.

The funny thing is that most of our fears about asking someone out are pretty baseless. No one is going to laugh at you or ridicule you for asking! The worst that can happen is that she says no and even when that happens, you are still actually better off than before you asked.

That is because the things we fear most are the things we know the least about. This is called fear of the unknown. Before you ask a girl out you have no idea what to expect. Your mind runs through all kinds of possibilities and we often blow everything out of proportion. The fact is, the more you do something, the more we learn and the more we learn the less we fear something.

In this book we are going to take you by the hand and go through some simple suggestions on how to make the entire process of asking a girl out as easy and successful as it possibly can be. The idea is that when you find out that you can be successful you will lose your fear and become more outgoing and adventurous when it comes to the other sex.

So let's just get started so you can finally ask that girl you have had your eyes on for a while out on a date. It's really a lot easier than you ever thought possible!

Who & Why?

I suppose the first thing we need to do is pick out the person and decide what it is about her that makes us want to see more of her and get to know her better. After all, there are differences in all of us and some things just resonate in our brains about a few particular people. Understanding what we like about that person can help us further along in the process.

Is there an emotional connection with this person? Do you get butterflies when you see her or when she walks in the room? Does she occupy your thoughts during the day? Or is it a physical attraction? Does she look gorgeous or sexy and you can't take your mind off of her? Whatever it is about her we should understand the attraction.

This book is about how to ask a girl out on a date. It is not a book on how to "pick-up" a girl for a casual sexual encounter or one-night stand. We are not her to discuss morals or value and what you do is up to you. But for the purpose of this book we are going to talk about how to meet, interact and ask out someone that you feel you would like to pursue a relationship with.

Now let's take a longer look at what you feel is special about this person. Knowing what you feel is special might help you navigate through the rest of the process. Understanding the attraction will usually uncover common things between the two of you. Our brains respond to people who like some of the things that we do and share the same beliefs, lifestyle and moral code. So if there are common areas between the two of you, we should know that.

The more information we have upfront the better we can approach anything in life and asking a girl out for a date is no different.

Do not Be Afraid or Intimidated

One thing many people, especially men struggle with is asking women who are very attractive out on a date. They feel that because these women are so attractive and so desirable that there is no way that they would possibly say yes to someone like them. So they just don't even ask and start looking elsewhere.

But the fact is, a lot of very attractive women, and also attractive men, are looking for the same thing in a partner that all other men and women are looking for. They value integrity over wash board abs and contrary to popular opinion men value honesty and nurturing over a huge chest or a pretty face.

Sometimes very desirable people, both men and women, find it difficult to find good people to ask them out because they appear so unapproachable that people are intimidated by them. This might be hard to believe but it is true. But these people, no matter how handsome or beautiful and no matter how wealthy they might be, want the same things that you and I want.

Another thing many men are afraid of is the competition they think they are going to face from other men when it comes to getting the attention of a beautiful woman. Average looking guys (that's most of us, hence the term "average") think they are not going to measure up against other men with better bodies, fuller heads of hair, or larger bank accounts.

But I am here to tell you to stop feeling sorry for yourself and stop thinking that someone else is better than you because they have more money to look better in a bathing suit or with their shirt off.

I am also here to tell you to stop thinking that a girl, any girl, is better than you because she looks good or has a great body. To think anyone is better than you is the same as thinking you are not as good as anyone else.

Let's stop comparing ourselves against other people. Let's stop thinking we don't have a chance because some girl is really good looking or really popular. Let's stop admitting defeat before we even take a single step towards asking her out. So many good women never get to meet the perfect man for them because of looks or because that person felt they didn't stand a chance.

Stop and think for a moment what you really have to lose by asking a pretty girl out for a date. She might say yes but she might say no. What is the worst that could happen if you get turned down? You just accept it and you move on. But at least you would have taken a chance and at least you would have tried.

That is better than going through life wishing you would have done this and should have tried that. Instead of going through life with regrets you might be going through life with the perfect woman just because you had the guts to take a chance where others did not.

In life good things come to people who go out and go for them. Good things go to the risk takers who gladly accept a little bit of defeat in order to grab a huge piece of success. Which one of those people are you going to be?

If there is someone you think is a bit out of your reach, shake it off and approach her. Do your best, try your best and look your best while you are doing it. Because chances are, that good looking girl is looking for the same things in life that you are looking for and it isn't washboard abs or a body that looks great in a bathing suit!

Gauging Interest

One thing that might make the entire process easier is to know whether or not there is any potential interest from the girl you are interest in. If you feel there is a mutual attraction then not only will she probably say yes, but you should be less nervous because the possibility of being rejected is much less as well. Anything we can do to reassure ourselves that things are most likely going to end well will make the entire process go easier. It's a mental thing but it really can help.

People show interest in several ways. There are physical gestures and emotional clues that people give off when it comes to how they feel about other people. If we can "read" these gestures then we can have a pretty good idea of how to proceed or whether we should proceed at all.

Here are a few things we might want to look for when it comes to whether or not another person might be interested in us:

If someone likes us, or at least thinks positively about us, they will appear to be interested in what we have to say. If another person is always attentive and / or asks you for your input or advice, that should be viewed as a positive sign. If they dismiss your input or don't listen to you at all, that might be a negative sign.

People who like another person will sometimes spend more time with them of near them. If she routinely comes over to you or approaches you while you are out in public then this might be her way of letting you know she is interested in you. Of course, if she is always around you every day she might be a stalker but that's a subject for another book!

People who like other people will chat them up or at least say hello or some other greeting when they see them. This is just their way of being friendly. But when it comes to the attraction between the sexes, a friendly and unsolicited greeting is a good sign. If you say hello and she ignores you, that is not a good sign. But if this only happens once it might be that she was distracted or didn't hear you. If it happens all the time, though, her message is clear.

Facial expressions provide a wealth of information when it comes to how people feel towards another person. If she smiles and her face lights up when she sees you, that's a great sign. If she frowns or looks bored, that's a bad sign. This is one of the easiest signs to read in other people.

If she makes eye contact with you, that is a very good sign. It shows that she is willing to interact with you even if it is just to say hello. But when people approaching you look away or look down, that is not a good sign. It means they are hoping not to interact with you for whatever the reason might be. However, and this is important, she might also be shy or nervous because she is interested and doesn't want to be rejected just as you often fear. So try and figure out if this is disinterest or shyness. If you aren't sure, don't factor this is at all.

If you approach someone and they take evasive action not to interact with you that is a bad sign. But if they go out of their path to come closer to you or to say hello, that is a very good sign. People usually do not go out of their way to approach someone unless they have an interest or because they want something. If they want something that will become evident in the following conversation. But if she comes across the street or across the office to say hello, that is a very good sign.

Try and gauge the quality and length of your conversations as well. Many people will smile and say hello to be polite even though they have no feelings or interest in you. But if you engage in a conversation and that conversation goes on for a while and the other person does not try and end it or get away, that is a very good sign.

Last, but certainly not least, physical contact is a very good clue when it happens. If she puts her hand on your shoulder or arm while talking, that usually indicates interest. If she holds out her hand to shake hands when she runs into you on the street that is another good sign. Physical touching is a strong signal. But for some people, they are very hesitant to make any physical gesture and if this does not happen should not be construed as a negative sign

At this point we should just be trying to figure out if there is any interest on the other side. We do not need to get into involved conversations or have people show clear and obvious intentions. But if there are obvious signs we should make note of them whether they are positive or negative. Then we can figure out whether or not we should move further into the process or just find someone new and start over. Of course, we might decide to just ignore everything and hope for the best. But that can be dangerous so I would advise against that.

Before we move on, let me say this about gauging interest:

We are looking for signs at this point and we should not expect people to make obvious and pointed moves to tell you they are interested in you. While this does sometimes happen, these signs need not be obvious or overt. Some people will actually flirt with you and make their intentions very clear. But others with the same feelings might not be so obvious because that is not who they are in life.

So don't expect the obvious signs but embrace them when they come your way. It is much easier to ask a girl out when you are 99.9% sure she will say yes. But don't wait until you get to that point because it might never come!

Doing a "Self Audit"

There is an old joke that goes "I wouldn't join any club that would have me as a member". When it comes to asking a girl out, you need to make sure that you are someone that other people would like to interact with and get to know better. That means being able to present yourself in the best possible manner.

I am not talking about being someone that you are not. First and foremost, honesty is the best policy when trying to establish any kind of relationship with someone else. But that does not mean that there aren't a few things that we can improve upon to make ourselves appear more desirable and valuable in the eyes of that special someone.

While dating someone based solely on looks is extremely shallow, a person's appearance usually help us create a perception about that person. That perception will exist until we are proven wrong. So like it or not, how we look plays an important role in that first impression or initial perception.

The best way for you to improve your overall presentation is to take a hard look at yourself in the mirror and be very honest about what it is that you see. Lying to yourself or trying to convince yourself that everything is perfect is not going to do you much good. But being honest with yourself will help you put together a "to-do" list of possible changes.

Another option might be to confide in a trusted friend or relative and ask them what they like and dislike about how you present yourself. Do not get mad or insulted when they tell you things you might not want to hear. You also do not have to act on everything they say or even agree with it. But you want them to be honest so you know what might need to be worked on.

Here are a few things you should concentrate on:

Always be neat and clean and wear clean clothes. You don't need to be a fashion plate or wear designer clothes. But everything you do wear should be neat and clean. This lets people know that you take pride in yourself and your appearance. Girls love that in a man.

Brush, floss and groom yourself. No one likes yellow teeth, bad breath or a disheveled appearance. This tells people you don't really care what you look like or what other people might think about you.

It is perfectly fine to be comfortable with who you are but you should still keep yourself well-groomed and keep your breath fresh and clean. After all, no woman wants to sit in a restaurant with a slob with bad breath!

Be confident and self-assured but not cocky. Women like men who are confident in whop they are but they usually can't stand the obnoxious jerk. Act confident but don't brag and be in control without being over bearing. Women want someone they can trust and rely on when they enter a relationship.

Have a good "Look". You don't need to look like a model or Hollywood star. But you should have a look that is good and current. Lose the 1960's bell bottoms and flower power t-shirt! Look like you are ready for anything and keep your look current. Check some of the fashion magazines if you want a little help in creating a better look.

Be happy and out-going instead of moody and withdrawn. People like to be around other people who make them feel better about themselves and life in general. People tend to flock to those other people who make their lives better and more fun. You want to be one of those people.

If there is something you feel is getting in your way when it comes to meeting women, think about what that might be. Once you figure it out, take steps to correct it if that is what you think you should do.

But make the corrections or changes because YOU want to make them. Do not make them because you think you might be able to convince someone to like you.

Before we move on, let's say something else about appearance and grooming. There is a difference between not going out with someone because they don't wear the latest or best clothes and not wanting to go out with someone because they have poor hygiene or other issues.

We should never judge a person by how they look. That gorgeous girl over in the corner surrounded by a bunch of guys might have a really bad personality or other issues while that shy girl with the dated clothes sitting by herself might be the perfect companion for you. Never judge someone by how they look. That is very shallow and will limit your ability to find a really nice woman.

But at the same time realize that first impressions do matter and you want to make a great first impression whenever possible. You want her to say "Yes!" and give you the opportunity to get to know you better. So sometimes we have to do a little bit of straightening up to make ourselves look better to the people we are trying to impress.

Adopt a Positive Body Language

Many people don't realize the effect of how they appear in the eyes of others will have on their overall success in life. When it comes to asking girls out on dates, how they perceive you will definitely play a role in whether they say "Yes!" or "No!" When it comes to appearance, body language is a huge part of how people perceive you.

Body language is the message your body sends to others. Body language involves your posture, mannerisms and other physical gestures and movements that give other people clues about how you are feeling and your overall emotional state.

For example, if you stand straight and proud, people will think you are confident and self-assured. But if you are slouching over and looking at the floor, you might appear weak, insecure and nervous. None of this might be accurate or even partially true but it does help people form their perception on people.

Most everyone, both male and female, like people who are confident and self-assured. When it comes to a female, they look for a male who is emotionally confident and strong. This is not the stereotype of a woman needing someone to protect her as that is no longer the case in society today.

But it is reasonable to think that a woman is going to look for someone who is confident and emotionally strong to complement her in their relationship. Both men and women look for signs of strength and stability in their potential relationships. This becomes even more important if that relationship starts to become a long-term relationship.

Body language tells people that you are either someone to be reckoned with and respected or someone who can more easily be manipulated and dismissed. Because of this we should be making sure our bodies are sending out the proper message to those around us. Not just females are want to ask out on a date but everyone else as well.

Make an effort to see yourself as others see you. Look in the mirror and see how you carry yourself as you stand and walk. Are you upright and proud or are you slouching and meek? Are you showing confidence or are you showing weakness? In other words, are you looking like the type of person that you would like to be in a relationship with? If you are not pleased with your body language it is likely that others won't be happy with it either.

Though entire books have been written on the subject, let's just talk about a few things you should do when it comes to your own body language so you will be sending the right message to the girls you want to meet:

First of all, stand tall and don't slouch. This shows strength. Do not lean in as this can be viewed as aggressive and you run the risk of violating her personal space and make her uncomfortable.

Walk proud and with a purpose. This shows confidence.

Develop a firm handshake. This shows confidence and assurance.

Look people in the eyes when you are talking. This shows honesty and integrity. Do not look all around you as this makes you look insincere and evasive.

Smile a lot. It shows confidence and also helps relax people.

Do not cross your arms over your chest. This is often viewed as a closed stance and sometimes combative.

Keep your hands out of your pockets. This can be viewed as boredom or anti-social behavior.

Relax your shoulders and don't hunch them up. This conveys self-assurance and a relaxed state.

As we have already said, body language is an important part of your overall presentation in life. If you feel that your body language is sending the wrong signals, or if you feel that people are getting the wrong impression of what you do and who you are, I suggest getting a book on body language and learn more about what you are doing.

Almost everyone can improve the message they are sending other people just be being aware of their body language. At the same time you are learning about body language you will also be learning how to become more successful in other areas of life as well.

Always be Respectful and Courteous

Another important thing to remember is that if you want to get a date with a nice girl you need to be a nice guy. That means treating people properly at all times and behaving in a manner that is attractive in the eyes of the opposite sex.

Women like men who are respectful and courteous not only to their dates but to everyone else as well. They like men who are respected not just for what they have accomplished but also because they treat everyone around them with dignity and respect as well.

In some respects, it appears that chivalry is dead and this has become a dog-eat-dog world out there. A lot of people have adopted the "me-first" mentality and this can be a real turn-off in the eyes of your date or the person you are trying to ask out. No one wants to spend time with an arrogant self-absorbed jerk who treats other people as sub-ordinate. So if you are that type of person, watch out because it might be a roadblock that will keep you away from finding that someone special.

This means being the guy who behaves himself in public and says "please" and "thank you" and knows how to get what they want without cursing or berating someone else in the process. While this might sound like an outdated or worn out ideal, the fact is that most people would still rather be in the company of a nice person than a self-absorbed jerk.

The other part of this is that people want to be able to relax with the people they are dating. If you ask a girl out and then behave in a way that is embarrassing or annoying to her, then she is not likely to go out with you again. Your goal should be to make the entire process a positive one and treating people badly does not reflect well on either of you.

It is not enough to just be nice to your date or the person you are out to impress. If you treat them nicely but they see you treating other people poorly, they will wonder which is the "real you" and then wonder if you are just one big phony, This sends mixed signals to the other person and this can stand in the way of the two of you getting to know each other better.

I am a firm believer in the old school approach where the man opens and holds the door for the woman and he also opens the car door and walks her to her front door as well. This is not chivalry or anything like that. It is just treating people the way they should be treated. In other words, it is just doing what is right and has been proven right for centuries.

Discovering Common Ground

One thing that is always difficult is finding something to do on your first date that both of your will enjoy. Not only that but finding out what to talk about especially at the beginning of the date is sometimes difficult as well. This is where finding some common likes or dislikes helps you to get through the awkward parts.

But finding common ground can also help you get a "Yes!" from a girl when you ask her out. If you have a common passion for something and you include that in your date, she might say yes because she knows she will enjoy herself on the date even if you do not turn out to be the man of your dreams!

For example, if you both love art and you ask her to go to a special exhibit in your town she might say yes because she wants to see the exhibit and those things are usually nicer and more enjoyable when you go with someone else. She also might think that even if the two of you don't hit it off, she will still get to see the exhibit. So in her mind this date has little downside.

Contrast that to asking her to go to the baseball game over the weekend. If she hates baseball and finds it boring, she might say no just to avoid having to sit through an entire baseball game. She might even like you but really hate baseball. So she might say no and you might never ask her a second time.

People make dating decisions based on figuring out the upsides and downsides of going out with someone. If there is more upside than downside, you will probably get a yes. If there is more downside than upside, you probably will get a no. It's not rocket science.

But even if she says yes, you have the challenge of finding things to talk about either on the date itself or getting to and from the date. You might spend the time at the art exhibit just looking but what about on the ride there or the trip home? You need to talk eventually and when those times come around, you need something to talk about.

Common ground or shared interests gives you both something to talk about that does not require either one of you to get overly personal with each other. You can keep the conversation light and enjoyable by discussing common interests and things you know will be of interest to both of you.

These common interests can also be used as ice-breakers that can lead to other discussions as you find out more about each other.

For example, if you go to the art show and she tells you about an exhibit she saw in London last year. That could open up a conversation on England or travelling or that particular exhibit. Now the conversation can get deeper as you both find out a little more about each other.

The other thing that works well for the guy is that when you make the effort to find some common ground it tells her that you care enough about her to find things to do or talk about that interest her. It is one thing to go to the car show and talk about your car for 5 hours and something else entirely to talk about something that is important to her.

Finding common ground can be very easy or very tricky. If you work with the person you want to ask out then you probably have talked a bit and know a little more about her from those conversations. Or, you can talk to a trusted co-worker (who can keep a secret) and ask them if they know something she likes or dislikes.

If you have met through a common friend then consider asking that person what she likes to do and just as important, things she does NOT like to do.

If you just met casually at an event, the event itself can be an ice breaker or be used to start a light conversation. For example, at the art exhibit you might ask her what she thinks of a particular painting or sculpture or even the entire exhibit. If you meet at a book reading, you can talk about the books you have read recently.

Sometimes we just meet someone on a bus or train and we feel some kind of emotional attachment. In those cases, she what she is wearing or carrying and see if you strike up a conversation about those things. Keep it light and go from there.

But once you find a common interest or passion, try and use that to pick the perfect date or to start that all-important first conversation. If you find something to talk about that is interesting to her, she will listen to you longer and you will have a longer period of time in which to convince her that you are a great guy that she should go out with.

Breaking the Ice

Part of the process of asking a girl out on a date is not scaring her off in the process. That means letting her know who you are, where you are from and why you would like to go out with her. It's a simple process but a very important one.

Imagine a total stranger coming up to you and asking you to go somewhere with them. You would likely be flooded with thoughts about serial killers or plots from a horror movie. But the reality is that there are people out there who are less than upstanding citizens so people must be on guard when it comes to meeting new people.

If you want to ask someone out, ask yourself if that person really knows who you are in the first place. Even if that person is at work they might be in another department and not aware of you at all. If the person you want to ask out lives in your building, don't count on her realizing you live there too. She might not know you even exist!

The first part of asking someone is called the ice-breaker or introducing yourself to her so she knows who you are. You might say something like "Hi! My name is Steve and I live on the 6th floor. I was wondering if you would like to go to a movie with me some time?"

In that statement you told her who you are, where she might know you from and what you wanted from her. At this point she can either say yes or no but at least she knows you aren't some strange weirdo on the street trying to go out with her.

The idea is to reassure her of who you are and that you have only the best intentions. You want to allow her to relax a bit and at least be open to the idea of going out with you. You might even let her know of some common ground the two of you might share.

For example, you might say something like "I'm Dave from the 4th floor and I play softball with a group of people from the neighborhood. I've seen you playing sometimes as well and was wondering if you would like to play with us on Saturday morning. We just play to have fun and it's a really great group of people."

There you mentioned who you are, let her know some common ground exists between you and also asked her if she wanted to do something with you that you already know she enjoys doing. From her point of view she might figure that she will have fun playing softball and she will meet some new people, including you, by accepting your invitation.

Think of breaking the ice as setting up the offer with some information designed to make the date sound as fun as possible while making her feel that you are someone with good intentions that she might want to get to know a little better.

Sometimes you might want to break the ice before you are ready to ask her out. If someone looks interesting you might just try saying hello to her a few times whenever you see her so that she is aware of you and knows you exist. Then, when you are ready to ask her out she already knows you because she has seen you frequently at work or in your building or neighborhood.

This is all about preparation and setting up the offer with a good background so she will be less leery of you and what you want. Sometimes it is all in the prep work and delivery. So take your time, break the ice, and ask that special someone out for what hopefully may be the first of many dates in the future.

Interact with Her

It is difficult to go up to a complete stranger and say "Would you like to have dinner with me?" If you try that you are likely to get turned down immediately and perhaps even be introduced to a can of Mace or pepper spray. Instead, we usually will have some kind of interaction with each other prior to asking her out.

Interacting with her does not mean you have to sit down and have a long and in-depth conversation with her. Interactions can be as simple as a few "Hello's" as you pass in the hall or when you see each other at work or at the supermarket. It's often not how you interact but that you interact at all with each other that counts.

For example, a nice lady moves in to the apartment next to you. So you see her coming and going a few times a week and you ignore her all the time. Chances are she will have noticed you and wondered why her next door neighbor is so stuck up or unfriendly.

Instead, when you see her smile and say hello. Tell her it is a nice day or that it's really cold out or anything that she will have to respond to.

Sometimes even just a smile when you see each other can work wonders. Every smile or comment is an interaction and helps you to become a little more comfortable with each other. The more comfortable she gets with you the greater chance you will have that she will go out with you. Every interaction makes you less of a stranger and more of a friend and that is exactly what you are shooting for at this point.

Interaction also provides an opportunity to get to know a little bit more about each other so you can decide if this person is right for you. Sometimes getting to know someone can help flush away that negative initial impression she has of you. Sometimes the more people find out about you the more they like you.

Interactions helps you break down barriers and reduces fear and suspicion. It gives you the opportunity to get the real you out and in front of her so she can see how special you really are. Learning how to interact with other people is a valuable skill to possess. But when it comes to dating and meeting new people, it is more than just a tool, it is a necessity.

All this being said, sometimes interacting with other people is a lot easier said than done. Maybe you are shy or just a bit intimidated by talking to girls. A lot of guys feels this way. If that is you then it is time to break down that barrier and reduce that fear right away. The only way to do that is to practice.

Make it your goals to interact with as many girls as possible during the next week. Smile at people you walk pass. Smile at the check-out girl and wish her a nice day. Talk to a few girls at work or go to a public event and practice talking to people. Gradually you will become more comfortable with the entire process and you can then try it with someone special when the time arrives.

If someone rejects your attempt to engage then just walk on by and try it with someone new. Eventually your nerves will calm down as your fear subsides. Then you will become more at ease and your delivery will appear less nervous and more polished. Think of this not as an individual exercise but as a work in progress.

However you choose to do it, just start interacting with more people every day. Try and place your shyness off to the side and start interacting with people and engaging them in conversations. You will be surprised how much easier several aspects of life will become once you allow others inside your social circle.

Help Her Out

One of the best ways to get to know someone is to help them out when they need help or a favor. This not only allows you to do a good deed but also allows the other person to see what a nice guy you really are.

For example, if you see a new neighbor loading her cart with all her possessions as she moves into your building, offer to give her a hand. You can then get to know each other as you carry things upstairs. You might even find common ground such as offering to cook her a dinner or take her out to dinner because she is new in town and has not stocked her kitchen as yet!

At work you might volunteer to be on a project she is on or offer to help her with something she is working on. This is especially useful when you possess a skill or talent that she doesn't really have but needs it for her project. You offer to help, you spend time together working on the project and both of you get an idea of whether there is anything there worthy of building a relationship on.

But be sincere when you help. Do not make it obvious that you are only helping so that you can advance your agenda. Do not make her feel that you are carrying large boxes up 6 flights of stairs just so she will go out with you. Use the opportunity for what it should be. A chance to help someone out while getting to know a little bit more about them.

Helping someone with anything in their lives make you almost always look better in their eyes. They will see you as someone who care about other people and is willing to sacrifice your time to help someone else out. This can be a very appealing quality in the mind of the woman.

Smile When You See Her

People like to feel happy and they like to feel good. Because of this we allow people into our lives that help us feel good and make our lives better. This also applies to who we date and why we date them. If they make us feel good, we'll date them. If they make us feel worse, we'll pass. It's not rocket science.

A smile makes people feel good. A smile is disarming and has a calming effect on the soul. If someone comes up to us and smiles, it makes us feel just a tiny bit better. Their smile means they are glad to see us. Their smile says they are happy and want us to be happy as well.

Smiles draw you in closer to other people. Smiles make us less guarded and more open to new people. If you walk up to two people and one is smiling while the other is frowning, you almost always want to hang out with the person who's smiling. It is just human nature to want to feel happier and better about life.

If there is someone you would like to date or get to know better, always greet them with a sincere smile. Make your smile your introduction. Allow your smile to allow them to relax a bit and let down their guard. A smile will prepare them to learn more about you and let you in a little bit closer.

Look Your Best

Contrary to popular belief, not all women are looking for rock hard abs and a chiseled physique. But most women are looking for someone who looks like they have their act together. In other words, they are looking for someone who cares enough about how they look that they will make an effort to look good in front of other people.

I often find it amusing, even down right incredulous, how people go out in public these days. I guess I am a little "old school" when it comes to how people should look but I think there are more people who feel exactly the way I do than the other way around.

That is because how we look speaks volumes about how we feel about ourselves. I see someone who is neat and clean and has their hair combed and I get the impression that this person has their act together. This is someone who cares enough about how they appear to others that they make an effort to look good at all times.

But if I see someone with their pants down around their knees or hair that is disheveled or has on dirty or smelly clothes and I think "there is someone who has very little price in how they look". Like it or not appearance matters.

Most people will dress up for a date or when they are out looking for someone to possibly date. People will dress way up when they are going to a club or to a nice restaurant. That is more the norm these days although I have still seen people in 5 star restaurants in old blue jeans! But just dressing up when you are trying to meet someone is dangerous.

Suppose you get dressed up and meet a nice girl but then you bump into her at the mall when you are wearing an old ripped t-shirt with your pants down to your thighs? Do you think she will be impressed? Do you think she is going to say to herself "Now THAT's a guy I want to date?"

I don't think so.

Take pride in the way you look at all times. After all, you never know when you are going to meet that special someone and you had better be ready to make the best of that situation. I'm not saying to go to the supermarket in a tuxedo but don't show up in old and dirt clothes and a smelly jacket either!

That also doesn't mean that you cannot take a quick trip to the home store in your work clothes to pick up a part for a project you are in the middle of.

In that context she might appreciate the fact that you are handy or know how to build stuff. The home center is full of people in work clothes. But not a five star restaurant.

The key is to always look appropriate for the place you are going. You should blend in and make cause people to look at you in wonder because of what you are wearing. People should not look at your 3 day beard because you didn't feel like shaving.

When you ask a girl out you want her to be comfortable with who you are. She is going to want to be seen in public with people who are neat and clean not people who haven't shaved or taken a bath in 2 weeks. This might sound like over the top but women want to be on the arm of a good looking man. They want someone they can introduce to friends and eventually family with their head held high.

Last, but certainly not least, is the fact that how we look, and how we take care of ourselves, is a direct relationship with how we feel about ourselves. Women want to date men with pride and self-respect. Most of the time those are the people who take the time to make sure they look good when they leave their home and go out in public.

As we said before, you don't have to wear expensive clothes and have expensive jewelry. But you do need to make sure that what you do wear is neat and clean and that your personal grooming is what it should be. Women don't expect perfection but they do expect someone who does care what they look like.

When You Can Date Without Asking Her!

The very best way to get a first date with someone is to choose an event where both of you will be attending anyway. That way you don't actually have to ask her out and be afraid of the possibility of rejection. You would be surprised at how many of these opportunities you can run into!

For example, if the girl you want to ask out and you work in the same office or company, attend a company event that you think she is also likely to attend. This can work out very well because you already have some common ground because you work for the same company. So use that as a starting point and go from there.

For those girls who are not part of your work team or company there could be community events, parties or meetings that she might attend as well.

These work out well because there will be a lot of people around so there will be little pressure on your to hold a long conversation if she is not interested or when you have little to talk about at first. As for common ground, well, you are at the same event, right? So just start there and see where things go.

If you know she has a particular interest or is a member of a certain club, then why not join that club or at least attend an initial meeting to check it out. There you might be a familiar face and you can use the club or activity as common ground or as an ice breaker. Sometimes this might also expose you to different activities as well as different people.

A perfect example of this might be if she is a member of a local gym or health club. Everyone should work out and keep themselves in shape and here you can not only get in your workout but get to run into her at the same time.

The one thing you really need to watch out for is trying to get too close or meet her in too many different place. If you are constantly following her and "accidently" running into her, she will be suspicious and probably a little freaked out as well. It might even land you in trouble with the law as well! Sometimes there is a fine line between trying to meet someone and becoming a stalker.

Common friends can also play a role if they are willing.

If they can make her part of a group and then get the entire group to go out for dinner, then you can become part of that group and get to know her a little better. If the friends think you two might be good for each other they could even invite each of you as singles and then because everyone else is a couple, you two would naturally talk to each other as being single in the group would be your common ground.

Meeting someone in this manner has its advantages. First, you do not have to actually ask her out and still get to meet her and learn more about her. Second, you do not have to carry the entire conversation for the evening as other people will be around and they will be talking as well. Third, you don't have the pressure of a one on one encounter so both of you will be more relaxed and easier to talk to.

But perhaps the best thing about a group meeting is that if things do not work out between you, there are other people around to talk to and interact with. Since this was actually not a "date" then there are no hurt feelings or expectations on either side. You can simply just walk away at the end of the dinner or event and not have that awkward task of exiting the date.

If you are really shy or nervous about asking a certain person out, this just might be the best way for you to see if this person has any interest in you and to find out if she is the type of person you would like to get to know better. There is a huge potential upside with very little, if any, downside.

Ask Her in Private

One mistake people usually make is asking a girl out when there is a group of people around. This usually doesn't work well because you have created a pressure situation because there are other people listening to or being exposed to the process.

Asking a girl out while she is with friends, co-workers or relatives puts her on the spot and might make her uncomfortable. She might be embarrassed or nervous and might not want others to know that she is interested in you. So out of embarrassment or fear she might say no. when that happens things become very awkward for both of you.

Another possibility is that if you ask her out while she is with other people she might not want to go out with you but is afraid to say no in front of other people and come off looking bad. So she might say yes only to call you the next day and cancel the date. Then she feels bad and you feel worse because you are excited that she said yes and were looking forward to the date.

If you want to have the best chances of an honest answer that is not influenced or directed by fear or nervousness, then find a private time or place to ask her out. If she is at work then maybe ask her at lunch or when you see her by herself and there is little chance of someone else dropping by.

If she lives near you or if she has a common interest that often brings you to the same place, then ask her after the event breaks up for the night and the crowd is dispersing. Or, if the night is going real well and you see there is definite interest, ask her whenever the conversation or situation gives you an opening.

If you are unsure about whether or not there is any interest on her part, consider waiting until the event or evening comes to a close and ask her on the way out. This way if she does say no there will not be an evening of awkwardness or hurt feelings hanging overhead. This is important if the event or situation does not include a lot of people.

Of course, if you have her phone number you can make the process very private by calling her when you know she is likely to be home. Try not to call her at work unless that is the only number you have for her. Remember that you want her to be able to talk openly and honestly and if you call her at work you have no idea who else might be around to listen to the conversation.

Asking someone out on a date is a somewhat personal process that has the potential to make one or both people uncomfortable at times. But handling this in a private setting reduces not only the pressure but the fear as well. Most of us can take rejection when it is done privately. But when we are rejected in the presence of a group of people that becomes much harder to deal with.

So find a private time to ask her out. If you pick the time and it runs out that she is with other people, consider postponing your invitation until a better and more private time should arise. You want to create the perfect time when there is the least amount of pressure on either of you. This could be the start of something great for both of you so it just makes sense to give it the best chances of success!

Create a Low Risk First Date

First dates can be a tense and nervous time for both of you. To improve your chances of getting that much sought after "Yes!" try and create a low risk type of date that is easy to agree to. That means finding something that has a very limited downside for her if she has some reservations about going out with you. Some people might have them and it is your duty to dispel them as best as you can.

After all, she really might not know you that well at all and there are enough jerks in this world that women are taught from day one to be suspicious of everyone and to protect themselves at all times. While it is sad that people are raised that way, it is the responsible thing to do in order to prepare oneself for the real world.

Because of all of this, a low risk date will give you the very best chance of success.

A low risk date is something where she will be able to relax and enjoy herself without fear. Usually a public place where she is surrounded by people is best. That is important because she doesn't really know you and you want her to feel safe and secure at all times. She will think that no one would try anything while surrounded by people.

Low risk is also something where she is not investing a lot of time. In fact, this is best for both of you. Going to a movie is good because while you will be in each other's company for a few hours you will be watching the movie most of the time and not talking to each other. The first time two people go out there is not a lot to talk about as you are both feeling your way around each other.

Along the same lines you might consider asking her out for a cup of coffee instead of going out for dinner. A cup of coffee could be an hour or it could go for a few hours if you two hit it off. This just takes more of the pressure off and allows both of you to just relax a bit more.

Low risk is usually someplace within a short distance of where she lives. This will make her feel more secure knowing that if things do not work out that she can just walk home. If you are going somewhere far away and things do not work out, then she has to figure out how to get home or suffer through an uncomfortable ride in silence.

Here are some examples of low risk dates:

Going out for a cup of coffee

A dinner at a local pub or restaurant. (Live music helps!)

Going to see a movie or play.

Going to a concert.

Going bowling

Any other activity that takes an hour or two. (Might a baseball or other sporting event if she is interested in that!)

Then we have the opposite which are the high risk dates. These are the dates where you spend a lot of time together and there is more pressure and concerns involved. These are also dates where it is difficult to cut them short if one or both of you is not having a good time or just wants to leave. Asking someone to do any of these as a first date is likely to get you turned down because of fear or uncertainty.

Here are a few examples of **high risk** dates:

Taking her on a cruise

Going away for the weekend

Spending the day travelling somewhere a few hours away.

Going to a romantic restaurant or resort

Low risk dates give both of you a chance to get to know more about each other without investing a lot of time, effort or money. They are also safer for both of you and eliminate many of the concerns or fears in her mind about going out with someone new.

So find someone you would like to get to know better and create a low risk date for that first date. Then take it slow and gradually move up to the more intensive dates that are likely to follow if the two of you hit it off.

Keep it Light, Fun and Pressure Free

Keep in mind that your first date should be fun, light and enjoyable. Nothing too intense and nothing controversial. This is a time for getting to know each other not a time to take risks, get involved in a cause or take part in a controversy. In other words, it should be a time for fun and relaxation and a little conversation.

Take her to see a light and funny movie. Stay away from sad or depressing movies or movies with a political or social message. You should be laughing when you come out not crying. The same goes for social events and other outings. Keep them light and fun and give yourself time to get to know each other before getting into each other's beliefs and values.

I would also stay away from anything that involves competition unless you are going to do something as a group with people you both know. But beating her in tennis, or her beating you, might not go over well as a first date.

One exception might be something like bowling that people do for relaxation and fun rather than a competition. But think carefully before making up your mind.

Choose something that makes her say to herself after the date "Gee, I had fun!" If she enjoyed your company and had fun on your first date then you might have a really good shot at a second date if that is where you want to see things headed. If she comes home sad because of a movie or upset because of a disagreement between the two of you it might be the end right then and there and you might never get a chance at a second date.

There should also be little or no pressure involved either. For example, if you decide to go to the amusement park, she might not be thrilled about going on the Ultra Godzilla Terror Coaster but might go anyway because she didn't want to say no. So you might place her in a position where she feels uncomfortable and not even realize it.

If you are taking her out to dinner or lunch (lunch is less pressure than dinner) then try and stay away from specialty restaurants and choose a place with a wide variety of food. She might not like Asian food or steak so if you take her to an Asian restaurant or a steakhouse, she will not have a good time. Instead, go to a restaurant where she will have a wide choice of food so she can enjoy both your company and her meal.

Your goals on that first date is to make sure that you do something where she has a good time. (It is better if both of you have a good time but concentrate on her experience first!) You also want to have the opportunity to get to learn a little bit more about each other in a very causal manner.

That might mean choosing a quiet restaurant where it is easy to hear each other as opposed to a crowded club where talking is difficult. The easier it is to hear the more you will talk and the more you talk the more you will learn about each other.

Take the pressure off of her as well by initiating the conversation. Talking to her will help her relax a bit and help set the mood for the date. Keep it safe by staying away from politics, religion and sex. Instead, tell her about yourself, where you grew up and a few interesting things about yourself.

But don't brag and don't be obnoxious. She will want to get to know you but she doesn't want to hear how great you are and be made to feel like she is blessed that you decided to ask her out. That kind of feeling will get you shut down really fast!

Which leads us perfectly into our next suggestion……

Make the Date Mostly About Her

Technically the first date is the time when both people want to learn more about the other person. But the truth really is, if you asked her out on the date you should make her feel needed and appreciated. One of the best ways to accomplish that is by making her the focus of the date. Put yourself second and focus on her for now.

Ask her open ended questions about herself and take an interest in the answers. Open ended questions are questions that usually cannot be answered with just a yes or no answer. They are questions that are designed to get people talking.

For example, if you are interested in what she does for a living (and you should) you might ask her if she likes her job.

But she might just say yes or no and nothing else. But if you ask her to tell you about her job, then she will have to tell you something about herself and her job. She really can't just say no. (Unless she is a top secret government agent sworn to secrecy!)

If you want to find out if she likes sports, you can ask her if she likes sports but she might say yes or no. But if you ask her what sports she likes or enjoys, she has to come up with an answer with some information in it.

Now you want to ask questions but you don't want it to seem like or feel like you are grilling her for answers. Between questions, or as a lead-in for a certain question, give her some information about yourself in the process.

For example, you might say "I play adult softball on the weekends. We have a great team and I have played with them for 5 years. Are there any sports that you enjoy?" This tells her a little something about you while asking her for a little something about her. After the exchange each of you knows or understands a little bit more about the other.

It is important to be interested in what she has to say. Turn the cell phone off and stop texting your buddies or checking the score of the big game. There will be more game but maybe not more dates if she feels you are not interested in her.

So when she talks, listen. Ask questions about what she is saying and add your own comments if you have similar experiences or interests. Make her feel that you value what she is saying. Everyone likes to feel appreciated and valued and one very effective way of accomplishing that is by just listening to what people have to say.

Don't interrupt her and never minimize or trivialize what she has done. If you have done something better or more impressive, keep it to yourself for now. There will be plenty of time for that later. For now, it should be all about her and making her feel valued, appreciated and important.

There will be plenty of time for you later.

But if she asks you questions, be honest without bragging. It is good to be proud of what you have done and another to be so full of yourself that it turns other people off. People don't like braggarts and they usually don't like to spend any more time with them than they have to. So if you brag a lot on date one, your next date might be a first date with someone else.

Be Honest!

We all want to make ourselves out to be the person the girl will really like and want to go out with. That is just human nature. But trying to be someone you are not is very difficult and will wind up causing you more trouble than you think it will. Your best strategy is to be who you really are and hope for the best.

It takes a lot of effort to tell a lie and even more effort to live that lie. People who lie constantly have to remember what they told who and then perpetuate that with further lies down the road. Dating is no exception to this rule. If you try and be someone you are not, it will not end up well.

For example, if she is a dancer and you tell her you love to dance even though you hate it, she will think she is doing something wonderful for you by constantly asking you to go to dance clubs. So you will spend more and more of your time doing something you hate because you told her you liked it.

The same goes for food. If she loves Italian food and you hate it, you best tell her you don't like it and hope that she accepts that and that it isn't a deal breaker. Otherwise you will find yourself going to many Italian restaurants and searching for something you can tolerate on the menu. All the time she thinks she is doing something you both love.

That being said, relationships are all about compromise and it should never be all one sided. You should do things that she enjoys and she should do things that you enjoy. But you should never pretend to enjoy something that you hate or that makes you feel uncomfortable or unsafe.

That is why it is so important to make the first date a very safe and generic date that almost everyone would enjoy or at least not mind doing.

But even before you ask her out, do not try and make yourself into someone you think she would like you to be. No one can live a life that is someone else's version and be truly happy about it. It is best to be honest upfront and have her say no than it would be to have her think you are someone you really aren't and have to live that life or lose her in the future.

Who Pays?

Today is so much different than it was when your parent or grandparents were your age. Back then men were expected to pay for most everything because it was the men who had the best or highest paying jobs while the women were homemakers.

Now men and women both hold high paying jobs and have successful careers. So the issue now is not who can afford to pay for the date but who should pay for it. Unfortunately there are no hard and fast rules for who pays but there are a few guidelines that might help you avoid this potentially awkward time in the date.

Generally speaking, whoever asks the other person out is usually expected to pay for that first date. That is another reason for making the first date a very generic event. First dates should never be expensive because the two of you are just getting to know each other and if you pull out all the stops on the first date and spend a fortune, she might expect the same next time. Plus spending a lot of money can make the women feel awkward.

So if you ask a woman out for a first date then you should expect to pay for whatever you do or eat on that date. You should pay the dinner or lunch check or pay for the movie tickets and buy the popcorn. If you don't think you can really afford what you planned on doing, then choose something else instead. Remember it is not so much what you do on your date but instead how you get to know a bit more about each other that counts.

If she offers to pay half the bill then it is up to you. Personally if the bill is not a large one I think the man should pay the entire check. This is not because the woman cannot pay but because she should not have to pay. Call it chivalry or being sexist but I just think it is the right thing to do.

If she asks you out on a date then she might expect to pay. At that point you can either let her pay or tell her you enjoyed her company so much you feel that you should pay. She may accept or decline your offer but your probably would have impressed her just by offering.

Sometimes the subject might come up earlier in the date such as when buying tickets or when ordering your entrée. She might state that she will pay for her ticket or food and it is up to you how to handle that offer. You can tell her you will pay or you can accept the offer. If she is insistent, do not argue. Instead, make a counter offer such as you will pay the check and she can leave the tip.

Or you will buy the movie tickets and she can buy the popcorn. This way you will pay the majority of the cost while allowing her to pay a smaller part.

If your first date happens to be a more costly event such as an expensive concert or other event she wants to go to, it is perfectly fine for each of you to pay your own way to the event. If you have a meal or drink afterwards, you should pick up that cost.

Who pays for what is part of the communication process that should develop between the two of you. It is perfectly fine to allow her to pay for a subsequent date if the two of you continue to see each other. Society has erased the notion that a man always pays but that doesn't mean the man should never pay.

Another factor might be when one of you earns much more than the other but in those cases you should tread very lightly. You do not want to say you will pay because you earn more money because that might make her feel bad or angry. It is all right to be generous but not all right to make someone feel inferior or inadequate in the process.

After Date Follow-Up

Throughout the date you will make certain judgments about the other person. As you learn more about her, you will eventually come to a conclusion that you want to see her again or that the two of you are not really made for each other and should not have a second or third date. Sometimes you might still be unsure and think a second date might be a good idea.

This is another area where it is best to be honest without hurting the other person's feelings. If you had a good time and would like to see her again, tell her you had a good time and will call her. If she responds that she would like that, you're good to go. If she says she doesn't think it will work out, act graciously and accept her decision. Hopefully she has the class to let you down gently and not be rude about it.

If it is you that doesn't think a second date is a good idea, you can tell her goodnight and see what her reaction or response might be. If you get the impression that she wants a second date and you are not interested, then tell her nicely that you don't think it is going to work out.

Hopefully she will accept it as graciously as you would have.

One thing you should never do is to take the easy way out and tell her that you will call her and then never call. She might have really liked you and is anxiously waiting for the call that is never going to come. That is not something that anyone should be put through. Exit the date with honesty and class.

If you had a good time there is nothing wrong with calling her the next day and thanking her for going out with her and telling her that you enjoyed your time together. Then you can take her lead and ask her if she would like to go out again. Don't pressure her and let her make her own decision. If she says yes, then plan a second date. If she says no then start the process all over with someone new.

The second date can be a little more private and last for a little longer period of time. At this point both of you know enough about the other to engage in some small talk and have also decided that there is enough in common between the two of you to give things a try. The nervousness might not be totally gone yet but the fear is probably a distant memory.

The important thing is to take things slow and never rush or pressure the other person. Allow the relationship to move ahead at its own pace whatever that pace might be. Men usually like things to move faster while women tend to be more cautious and show more restraint. Neither is the right or wrong approach.

We all need to do whatever we feel is right for us. And we need to be supportive and understanding when the other person wants something to move faster or slower.

But make sure not to smother her with attention and constant requests to go out. People want and need their space in life especially when just starting a new relationship. Limit your request and gestures like flowers or other things so that she will be happy about them instead of worried that you are crowding or pressuring her.

As we said in the very beginning of this book, this is not a book about one-night stands. Instead it is a book on how to ask someone out for what could be the beginning of a long-term or serious relationship. These relationships are built slowly over time and involve many dates and many different experiences. Relationships are a process where both people gradually learn more and more about each other. That is why honesty is so important in a long-term relationship.

So if the first date leads to a second date, remember what got you that coveted "YES!" in the first place and keep doing the same things. It will serve you well.

But if the date doesn't go well, do not despair. Because simply going through the process of asking someone out and going on the date will give you experience that will help you the next time and times after that. Almost no one is successful all the time but that doesn't mean you have to lose all the time either!

Why Rejection is No Big Deal

Not everyone is meant to get along with everyone else. You are going to meet people that you really like and some that you just cannot stand. Most of the people you meet will fall somewhere in the middle. So you are going to have to put yourself out there and meet people until you find the one that's right for you. It might happen on the first time or maybe the twenty first time.

People usually fear rejection because they imagine all kind of negative feelings and consequences that may not even be there. When this happens they make the rejection far more serious than it ever would be in real life.

Think about what would happen should the girl say no. If you followed the advice in this book and asked her privately, then the only one who would know would be you and her. Unless she was a big jerk and told all her friends, there would be a moment of mild awkwardness and then it's over. You would simply pick up where you left off with someone new.

Rejection is part of life and we all experience it multiple times. No one goes on a job interview and gets every job they want. No one plays sports and winds all the time either. Granted some of us win a lot more than others but even champions experience defeat every once in a while.

The most important part of rejection is not the rejection itself or the supposed pain it might cause but rather how we deal with it and move on in life. If you ask someone out and they say no and you repeat the same line over and over again and always get a no that is not good.

But if you get rejected and learn from the experience and refine your approach, you will have become a better person in the process. That is where the secret lies. Go out and ask that special girl out and learn from the experience. Learn how to become more confident and more polished. Confidence comes only after you experience success and you cannot experience success if you give up before you get started.

Even taking things to the extreme, if you ask someone out and they say no, the sun will still rise the next morning and you will still be walking around on this earth. There is someone out there for everyone and it is up to you to go out and find her. It might take a few trics, it may involve a few mistakes but she is out there. All you have to do is keep looking until you find her.

Then go and ask her out.

I just bet she will say yes.

And then there will be no more first dates. Just a second and a third and a………….

Dating Tips, Hints & Suggestions

1) Find someone to ask out for the right reasons. Looks and beauty are only skin deep. There is much more to a person than what shows on the outside.
2) Be nice and pleasant and ask her to do something you know she will enjoy.
3) Always be neat, clean and well groomed. Women appreciate that in a man.
4) Be on-time and make her the priority.
5) Make her laugh. We all like people who make us smile and laugh.
6) Be confident and vulnerable at the same time. That's called being human.
7) Help her relax. It will make things go better for both of you.
8) Be careful dating people you work with. If the relationship ends you still have to see each other at work.
9) Sometimes the best person is someone you think of as nothing more than a friend.
10) The more you share with someone, the closer you will become.
11) Choose a first date where there is something else going on to help fill the dead spots.
12) If you take her out to eat, choose something easy and clean to eat.

13) Keep some parts of you to yourself. A little mystery is always a good idea.
14) Be honest while respecting her feelings.
15) Treat her like you would want her to treat you.
16) If there is something you can do to make yourself look or feel better, do it!
17) Don't think anyone is out of your league. You'll never know until you ask!
18) Contrary to what you see in the movies, most people don't hop in the sack on the first date! Take it slow. Intimacy will come.
19) If she looks good, tell her. If she doesn't, keep that to yourself!
20) Win over her friends with your charm. Women do talk to each other you know!
21) Just be yourself. Most of the time that will be all you need!
22) Keep it simple at first. There is too much pressure in the rest of her life.
23) Don't push things to go too fast. Good relationships take time to build.
24) Ask her out for the right reasons. If your intentions aren't honorable, don't ask her out.
25) If in doubt, ask her out! You never know what might happen!
26) Don't let fear of rejection hold you back. There are too many good women out there.

For more books on interpersonal relationships and many other self-help topics, please go to our website at:

http://www.26ways.com

Printed in Great Britain
by Amazon